CLASSIC LANDFORMS OF THE

EAST DORSET COAST

D1381632

We should like to acknowledge the friendship, advice and information that we have received over the years, notably from Alan Carr, David K.C. Jones, David Horsfall, Geoff Poole, Bob Allison, Tim Burt, Eric Bird and Malcolm Bray. This edition is dedicated to them.
Andrew Goudie and Denys Brunsden

CLASSIC LANDFORMS OF THE

EAST DORSET COAST

ANDREW GOUDIE AND DENYS BRUNSDEN
University of Oxford and
King's College University of London

Series editors
Rodney Castleden and Christopher Green

Published by the Geographical Association
in conjunction with the
British Geomorphological Research Group

Geographical
Association

PREFACE

Geomorphologists study landforms and the processes that create and modify them. The results of their work, published as they invariably are in specialist journals, usually remain inaccessible to the general public. We would like to put that right. Scattered across the landscapes of England and Wales there are many beautiful and striking landforms that delight the eye of the general public and are also visited by educational parties from schools, colleges and universities. Our aim in producing this series of guides is to make modern explanations of these classic landforms available to all, in a style and format that will be easy to use in the field. We hope that an informed understanding of the origins of the features will help the visitor to enjoy the landscape all the more.

Encouraged by the success of the first edition of the Classic Landform Guides we are pleased to introduce this new edition, enhanced by colour photographs, new illustrations and with the valuable addition of 1:50 000 map extracts by kind permission of the Education Team, Ordnance Survey. The relevant maps for the area covered in this booklet are the Ordnance Survey 1:50 000 Landranger sheets 194 and 195; please refer to the current Ordnance Survey Index for 1:25 000 availability.

Rodney Castleden *Roedean School, Brighton*
Christopher Green *Royal Holloway, University of London*

Safety

The sea cliffs and rock slopes of the entire area are very precipitous and subject to rockfall. They are extremely dangerous and must not be climbed. Rockfalls do occur from the promontories and from the chalk cliffs.

© the Geographical Association 1997
As a benefit of membership, the Association allows members
to reproduce material for their own internal school/departmental use,
provided that the copyright is held by the GA and that the user acknowledges
the source. This waiver does not apply to Ordnance Survey mapping, questions
about which should be referred to the Ordnance Survey.
ISBN 978 1 899085 28 6
This edition first published 1997, reprinted 1999.
Published by the Geographical Association, 160 Solly Street, Sheffield S1 4BF.
The views expressed in this publication are those of the author and do not necessarily
represent those of the Geographical Association.
The Geographical Association is a registered charity no. 313129.

CONTENTS

Cover photograph: Lulworth Cove © Sillson Communications, Wareham.
Frontispiece: Old Harry Rocks, Isle of Portland © Sillson Communications, Wareham.
Acknowledgements
The authors would like to thank the cartographers of the School of Geography
(Peter Hayward of Poole, and Ailsa Allen) for drawing the original illustrations.
We also thank the many students we have taken to the area for their hard work and
penetrating questions.
The Geographical Association would like to thank those individuals and organisations referred
to in figure captions for their permission to reproduce illustrations in this publication.
Mapping reproduced from Ordnance Survey 1:50 000 Landranger mapping with permission
of The Controller of Her Majesty's Stationery Office © Crown Copyright 82324M 06/96
Copy editing: Rose Pipes
Illustrations: Paul Coles
Series design concept: Quarto Design, Huddersfield
Design and typesetting: Armitage Typo/Graphics, Huddersfield
Printed and bound in China through Colorcraft Limited, Hong Kong

INTRODUCTION

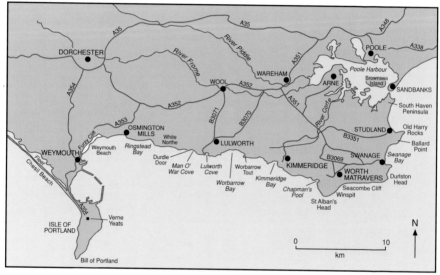

Figure 1: Location and access map of area.

As well as being one of the most beautiful and spectacular coastlines in the world, the Dorset coast (Figure 1) is also of great scientific importance to geologists and to those who study landforms – geomorphologists. To those people interested in landscape, the coast is perhaps best known for its variety of rocks and famous fossil localities, but visitors are invariably struck by the equally impressive, though not so widely explained, landslides, beaches, caves, dunes, natural arches and other coastal landforms. The purpose of this book, therefore, is to provide a concise description and explanation of some of the most important of these features on the coastline between Portland and Poole Harbour. A companion guide to the dramatic coastline of West Dorset, published by the Geographical Association, is also available.

This portion of the coast has been chosen because it is the best place in the British Isles to demonstrate the relationships between rocks and relief, the difference between concordant and discordant coastal landforms, the nature of problems involved in the construction of landform evolution models, the role of sea-level change, and the development of landslides.

THE PORTLAND CLIFFS

The coastline of the Isle of Portland (Photo 1) is composed of Kimmeridge Clay overlain by the Portland Sand, Portland Stone and Lower Purbeck Beds (Table 1). There is almost continuous rock exposure around the island's coast but much of the surface has been quarried. In England, Portland Stone has long been a very popular building stone due to its particular properties: it is a **freestone**, can be easily shaped and cut and is reasonably durable, except when it originates from the surf abrasion zone. Immediately under the Portland Stone are the Portland Sands which include clays, a thick sequence of **glauconitic** sands and cement stones. The underlying Kimmeridge Clay is an **overconsolidated** sequence of limestones, shales and clays which alternate rapidly and, in several horizons, have a high organic content and sometimes high oil content. They form the lower slopes around the northern part of the island but are rarely visible because they are covered in landslipped debris and quarry

Photo 1: The Isle of Portland. Photo: Sillson Communications, Wareham.

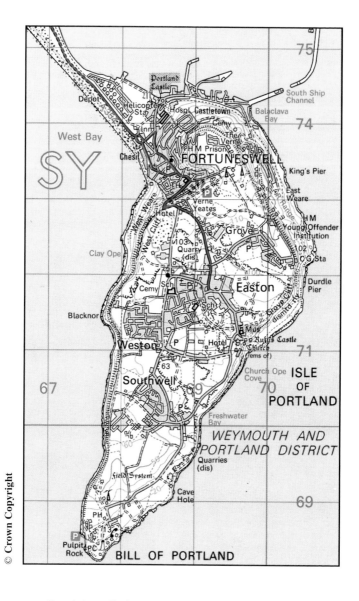

© Crown Copyright

wastes. Overlying all these are the lower Purbeck Beds, an easily erodible sequence of marls, thin limestones, shales and clays.

Figure 2 shows the Isle of Portland in its wider structural setting. Portland forms the southern flank of the north-west tip of the Shambles syncline and the island rises up-dip to form the southern limb of the *en echelon* Purbeck and Weymouth anticlines. The rocks dip to the south at the Verne but the dip swings south-south-east at 2.5° as the Bill is approached. The surface of the island also slopes to the south from an elevation of 135m to 15m but with a pronounced depression in the centre (Figures 3a and 3b).

Table 1: Main geological formation in Dorset

Era		Formation	Thickness (m) at coast
LOWER TERTIARY		Charma Sand	8
		Barton Clay	26-60
		Boscombe Sand	70
		Branksome Sand	70
		Poole Formation	160
		London Clay	30
		Reading Beds	30
CRETACEOUS		Upper Chalk	200-260
		Middle Chalk	34-56
		Lower Chalk	14-45
		Upper Greensand	30-42
		Gault	5-15
		Lower Greensand	20-60
		Wealden Beds	420-700
UPPER JURASSIC		Purbeck Beds	39-90
		Portland Beds	45-70
		Kimmeridge Clay	530
MIDDLE JURASSIC		Corallian Beds	60
		Oxford and Kellaway Clay	230
		Cornbrash	7
		Forest Marble	75
		Upper Fuller's Earth (Frome Formation)	38
		Fuller's Earth Rock	8
		Lower Fuller's Earth	45
		Inferior Oolite	6
LOWER JURASSIC	**Upper Lias**	Bridport/Yeovil Sands	90
		Down Cliff Clay	21
		Junction Bed	4
	Middle Lias	Marlstone Rock Bed	0.6
		Thorncombe Sands	27
		Down Cliff Sands	20-30
		Eype Clay	60
		Three Tiers	10
		Green Ammonite Beds	34
		Belemnite Marls	23
	Lower Lias	Black Ven Marls	46
		Shales with Beef	25
		Blue Lias	32

Source: *Bird 1995.*

Portland is the most instructive place in the British Isles to demonstrate the effect of geology on the distribution and form of landslides. Consider the following controls:

1. The rocks consist of a cap-rock of resistant but strongly jointed limestones loading onto permeable sands, sandrocks and clays. Water is thus able to move downwards to the **aquicludes** where it builds up high pore pressures and provides all the classic conditions for landsliding. There are several possible failure levels in the Kimmeridge as well as the Portland Clay and the clays may also slowly deform in a ductile manner.

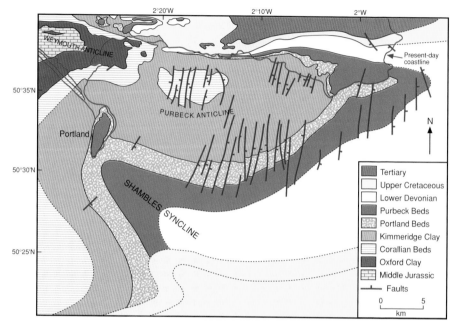

Figure 2: The structural setting of the Isle of Portland showing the control exerted by the Weymouth and Purbeck anticlines, the Shambles syncline and the Purbeck monocline. After: Donovan and Stride 1961.

2. The dip of the rocks is south to south-south-east which allows water to drain across the island from the highest to lowest points with a considerable head (Figure 3c).

3. The rocks, particularly the Portland Beds, are strongly jointed with master and conjugate joint sets running north-west to south-east, north-east to south-west, north to south and east to west (Figure 3d). They are controlled by the east to west axis of the Purbeck anticline and the north-west to south-east Shambles syncline. These joints allow the easy ingress of water and form weaknesses that dominate mass movement processes. The master joints are very influential and, as Figure 2 shows, they closely parallel the north-north-east to south-south-west fault patterns of the Purbeck anticline which should, therefore, be regarded as a major regional landform control.

4. The island is shaped like an elongated triangle aligned north-north-east to south-south-west. It has a very straight and angular coastal outline which, in places, exactly fits the master and conjugate joint directions (Figure 3d). The tops of the cliffs are vertical due to these joints. The structure thus seems to dominate the shape of the island at all scales and for all processes.

5. The rock sequence, dip and joint systems mean that there is a maximum thickness of Kimmeridge Clay exposed at the northern end of the island. This diminishes to no exposure at Tar Rocks

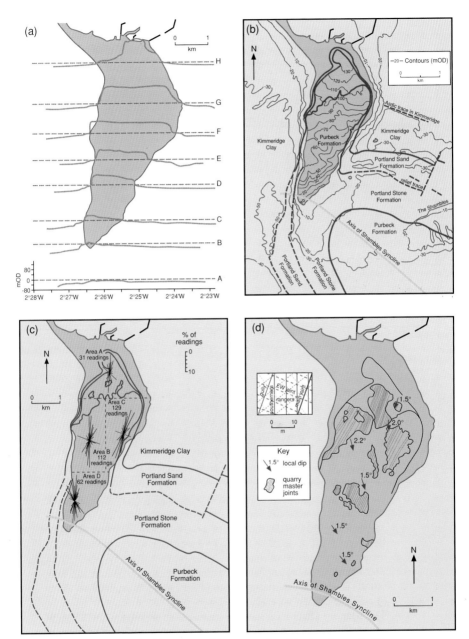

Figure 3: Isle of Portland (a) *topographic cross-section*, (b) *subsurface and offshore relief*, (c) *structural dips, and* (d) *master joint system.*

(SY 681724) on the west and Church Ope Cove (SY 698710) on the east. This was of course different during the Pleistocene glaciations when sea-level was lower and the Portland Sand-Kimmeridge sequence was exposed further to the south

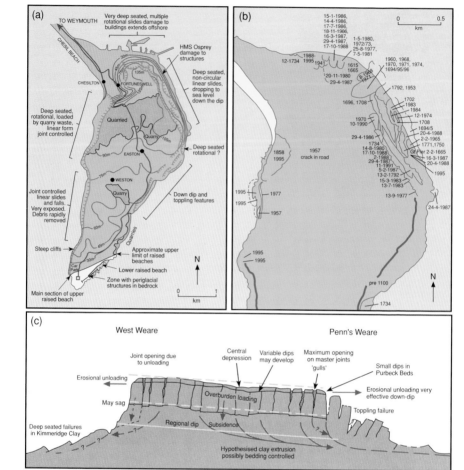

Figure 4: Isle of Portland: *(a) types of slides on the coast, (b) dates of recorded landslides, and (c) hypothetical section of lateral extrusion as a landslide mechanism.*

(Figure 3b). This was also the time of a colder, wetter climate when evaporation rates were lower.

6. The steep, exposed, coasts provide relief energy of greater than 60m (135-60m) for three-quarters of the island. Even the low cliffs of the Bill itself are nearly vertical.

7. The western cliffs face the full fury of the maximum-fetch winds of the Channel coast with deep water offshore and a total loss of loose debris at the foot of the cliffs. The eastern side faces less frequent short-fetch but powerful winds which also cause rapid erosion when erodible materials are exposed under the ramparts of fallen Portland boulders.

8. There has been considerable human interference of the cliffs, especially at West Weare (SY 683725), East Weare (SY 702730) and Grove Cliff (SY 702714) where huge volumes of quarry waste

Photo 2: Landslides on Portland *at (a) West Weare, and (b) East Weare.*
Photos: Andrew Goudie.

have been thrown over the cliffs to form scree slopes and to load the landslides at their heads. Large volumes of rock have also been quarried from these lower slopes.

These facts allow us to make a series of deductions about the evolution of the coastal landslides (Figure 4). First, they vary in size from the north to the south because of the available relief and clay exposure. Second, the heads of the slides lie closer to sea-level toward the south because the failure surface clays are descending on the dip.

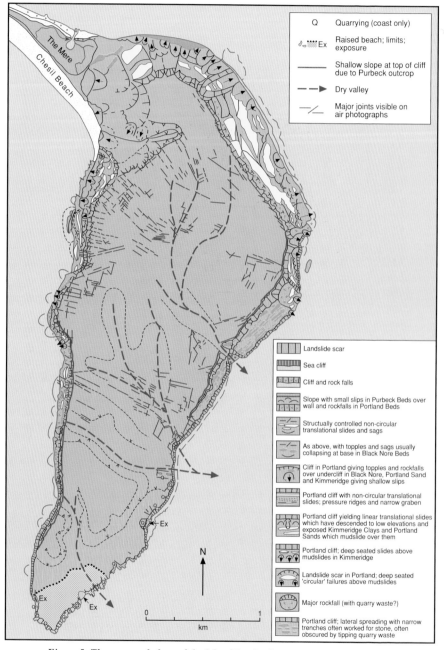

Figure 5: The geomorphology of the Isle of Portland.

The toes of the slides are known to extend offshore and it is a reasonable proposition that the slides initially occurred at the height of the last glaciation, with lower sea-levels and wetter conditions.

They are also known to have been influenced by human activity, as witnessed by Southwell in what may be one of the earliest records of humans in the role of geomorphological agents:

'On February 2nd 1665 the great pier was quite demolished and filled up with rubbish; and rocks that lay 40 yards off in the sea or the pierhead were risen up above the water, so that there were no hopes of making good that pier again; and the ways leading from the piers to the quarries were turned upside down and sunk in several places at about 30 feet. The north pier was cracked but might be repaired. The coast slid into the sea between the two piers, near 100 yards, and continued to do so ... It is conjectured this was occasioned by a great quantity of rubbish thrown over the cliff upon a clayish foundation, which was softened by the violence of the rain, and gave way, and not by earthquake as some imagined' (Southwell 1717).

Third, the type of slide changes around the island (Figure 4a). In the north, at West Weare, Castletown Dockyard (SY 690744) and above Balaclava Bay (SY 688742), there is maximum elevation, considerable exposure of Kimmeridge Clay, deep water offshore and an anti-dip orientation. The significant structural control is therefore the vertical jointing and the failure type is deep-seated and rotational. At West Weare (Photo 2a) the slides consist of multiple, joint controlled slices. At Castletown they are multiple rotational. Both also have their toes beneath sea-level. At East Weare the orientation of the coast is aligned north-north-west to south-south-east parallel to the dip. The elevation of the topography and the available shear surfaces descend down-dip. The dominant form is a series of *en echelon*, elongate and interlocked joint-bound slices becoming lower in elevation toward the south. There are indications of non-circular behaviour with sagging failures from the cliff; **grabens** and level-topped settling blocks at the head and rotation at the toes.

The landslides completely change their character when the coast changes direction to north-east to south-west between Durdle Pier (SY 705717) and Freshwater Bay (SY 691701). The cliff is now unsupported and down-dip. With deep water offshore and north-east to south-west master joints exactly parallel to the coast there is nothing to stop slides from developing and there is a maximum head of water available from Fortuneswell (SY 687736). The results are spectacular low lying complex slides and translational mudslides below Rufus Castle (SY 697712) at Penn's Weare, and perfect examples of toppling failures at Southwell Landslip (SY 678705) (Photo 2b). Although the subsurface details are unknown it is likely that the two areas are different. The Penn's Weare site seems to be slipping on a surface in the Kimmeridge. The Southwell site may be failing on the top of the Kimmeridge and at the southern end, this may involve the Portland Clay which is close to sea-level due to the dip of the rocks (Figure 2).

The origin of the central depression

The centre of the Isle of Portland has a noticeable depression which runs for 2km south of the Verne. It is drained by a very small stream and dry valley system (Figure 5). The relief is no more than 10m but a striking fact is that the local dip is very variable at low angles. It has been reported that the dip may become horizontal or even dip north-west, opposite to the regional dip. It is also noticeable that the master joints and associated gullies vary in their degree of openness, and are often very wide toward the east coast and closed tight toward the depression centre. These features made it easy to remove building stone and so contributed to the success of quarrying operations; unfortunately, however, they have never been systematically recorded. Related features that the island is noted for are the non-solutional caves, many of which, on the east coast, have been infilled to prevent the escape of prisoners working in the quarries! The phenomena are not universal nor is there a consistent pattern but all the quarries show distorted bedding and variously open, collapsed and infilled fissures.

Another significant feature is that the Kimmeridge Clay, when exposed, is often distorted, squeezing up and associated with columns of Portland Stone which show all the signs of having subsided into a ductile underlayer. These features have been described as being due to the lateral expansion of the cliff due to the extrusion of the underlying clays under the overburden weight of the limestone (see Brunsden *et al.* 1996). It has also been noticed that shear zones can be developed by the clay extrusion, sometimes along the bedding, and that these may subsequently be utilised as a control for the basal landslide shears.

The observed features of Portland satisfy many of the criteria described but there is, as yet, no sub-surface confirmation of shears, creep or surface subsidence. In applying the hypothesis, however, it is necessary to recognise the influence of the regional dip on the pattern of the features. The dip is to the south-east at 1.5°. It is reasonable to suggest that any clay extrusion would preferentially take place in this direction and that there would be more open gulls to the south-east. Columnar toppling and sagging, major landslide ridge displacement, foundering into a ductile layer and clay bulges would preferentially occur along any portions of coast orientated along the strike and down-dip.

All of these features are satisfied along the Great Southwell, Church Ope Cove, Rufus Castle, Shepherds' Dinner section of the Portland coast. Geologists also point out that it is difficult to match the exposures of clay on either side of the island. This may well be because of clay extrusion and deformation.

The hypothesis is tentatively put forward, therefore that some of these features of the Portland landslides can be explained by the overburden-loading/clay-extrusion lateral spreading model (Figure 4c).

Landslide activity

The activity of the slides is largely controlled by the erosional energy at the base of the slope, including excavation, but also by the disposal of quarry waste. On the west coast, facing the south-west gales, the cliffs between the Bill and Blacknor (SY 678715) are steep and dangerous and there is rapid removal of slip and rockfall debris. At West Weare, slides and rockfalls are currently active and causing concern because they are undercut and loaded by quarry waste. Movements of this type have been known at Fortuneswell from 1858 but at West Weare they are also caused by cliff undercutting and seem to be increasing in frequency. Cliff falls occurred in 1957, 1977 and in February 1990 (Figure 4b). At East Weare slow movements have been occurring for a very long time. Landslides are known to have taken place in this area in 1615, 1665, 1694-95, 1708, 1734, 1750, and in 1792 (when there were four), many of which seem to be related to loading of pre-existing slides by quarry waste thrown over the cliffs. The movements continue today and some of the Naval buildings are showing distress. Further south, natural slips occurred at Southwell in 1734 and at Rufus Castle before 1100. At Castletown Dockyard and the housing above it there are obvious signs of failure. Many houses have been demolished and rebuilt where they lie across the marginal shear surfaces and there is damage to the larger Naval buildings. These slides appear to be very old but still moving and it is interesting to speculate whether the movement has been assisted by dredging for the harbours at the toe.

Overall, the landslide story is a dramatic one which demonstrates perhaps better than anywhere else the principle of the adjustment of process and form to geological structure. Arguably, this is the hallmark of the Dorset landscape.

Access and safety

The landslides are not easy to visit and considerable care must be taken to avoid dangerous and exposed situations. The slow movements and deep-seated slides of the north are mainly inside the Naval base. The cliffs of West Weare and the scar of the Castletown slide can be seen from Chesil Beach and by scrambling on the shore. You are strongly advised not to view these slides from the top of the cliff or from close in at the cliff base where there is the danger of falling rock. As reported in the local newspapers in 1990: 'the whole of the cliff face from the end of the sea wall to Clay Ope is on the move and huge cracks have opened up on the face of the cliffs along West Weare'. The best sites to visit are Penn's Weare, where a descent to the beach can be made, and Southwell which can be easily visited from Portland Bill car park.

THE PORTLAND RAISED BEACH

Photo 3: The Portland Raised Beach. *Photo: Andrew Goudie.*

The raised beach at 15-16m above mean sea-level at Portland Bill (SY 677681) is perhaps the most important exposure of this type on the coastline of southern England (Figures 4a and 5). The section (Photo 3) is best seen by following the wire boundary fence of a small Ministry of Defence installation on the very edge of the sea cliff immediately to the west of the large car park.

At the top of the main section is a dark-brown stratified soil which is believed to contain windblown silt, called loess. Immediately beneath is a classic example of what is called **head.** This is a mass of angular, probably frost-shattered debris of local Portland and Purbeck limestone (up to 20cm long) set in a fine, silty matrix of yellow-brown colour. The head is crudely bedded with a shallow inclination of 5-10° to the south. Three layers have been identified (measurements are from the underlying shore platforms upward):

2.2-3.4m   Silty head and angular limestone pieces, showing considerable disturbance.

0.8-2.19m   Silty head with scattered limestone pieces and shells.

0.5-0.79m   Very silty head with only a few angular stones. Shelly.

Elsewhere on the Isle remains of mammoths, woolly rhinoceroses and other mammals, possibly including reindeer, indicate that sub-Arctic conditions existed when this material was being formed. The snail fauna recovered from the head is characteristic of grassland with areas of marsh and small pools. The snails indicate a cool but not cold climate. The suggestion that the climate was considerably cooler than today is supported by the way in which the upper parts of the head are disturbed into swirls and **involutions.** Geomorphologists usually associate these with the churning of soil under **periglacial** conditions caused by seasonal melting of frozen ground. Under such conditions, this head material can move downslope by a process called **solifluction.**

Beneath the angular head there is a fine loamy deposit up to 0.5m thick. This is light-brown in colour and composed of a very silty sand containing small calcareous pellets. There is some rolled pebble material in the bottom 20cm. It is believed that this deposit may have been laid down in a brackish coastal lagoon behind a stormbeach, possibly similar to the Fleet behind Chesil Beach.

The loam rests on a deposit of rounded pebbles, slightly cemented together by calcium carbonate, in which all of the typical features of a shingle beach can be clearly seen. The pebbles are mainly flint, local limestone and **chert**, comparable to those found on modern Chesil Beach though at a much higher level. There are also unusual stones that appear to have travelled much further, including materials from Dawlish, Budleigh Salterton (Devon) and Cornwall. Part of the deposit is much finer, containing whole and broken shell fragments. These have retained their colour and are well preserved. Geomorphologists believe that the shell creatures lived on a rocky shore in a sea whose temperature was only slightly colder than that of today.

At the base of the shingle, which is approximately 3m thick, there are many large rounded limestone boulders cemented onto bedrock and containing large fossil shells. These boulders, and some of the layers in the shingle, lie partly on top of one another like the tiles on a roof, and are tilted downslope toward the sea. This is a characteristic feature of pebble beaches and is called **imbrication.**

If one traverses (very carefully) around the wire fence to its limit and looks back at the main deposit, it is possible to view the bottom of the beach, which is a sloping rock platform, curving upwards to make the beginning of a cliff. This is a shore platform upon which the beach was deposited.

There is considerable debate and uncertainty about the age of the raised beach. The current viewpoint is that the beach represents a shoreline at about 14.5m above present sea-level. A technique called

amino acid racemisation seems to indicate that it may be as much as 210 000 years old and dates back to an interglacial when sea-levels were high because of the melting of water from the great ice caps. It is also possible, however, that some local tectonic uplift may have played a role in elevating the beach to its present level.

On the eastern side of Portland there are some other raised beach deposits at a lower level (6.95-10.75m above present sea-level) and these have been dated by amino acid techniques to about 125 000 years old. This means that sea-level was relatively high during the last interglacial (c. 120 000 BP) (Figure 6).

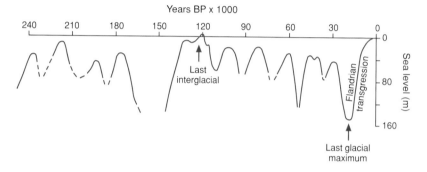

Figure 6: Sea-level change over the last 250 000 years.

Beneath the eastern raised beach, displayed on the other side of the Bill immediately behind the cafe north-north-east from the lighthouse, there is a fascinating section that may indicate the existence of a cold phase before the last interglacial. Here, at the base of the raised beach gravels, the shore platform is heaved, cracked and warped to a depth of up to 3m. The meticulous observer will also be able to reconstruct crude polygons of angular boulders which stand on edge. Such features are thought to be caused by frost action under cold conditions and are commonly known as periglacial (tundra) patterned ground and, more specifically as rock blisters. Since these are under the beach they may well be regarded as dating back to before the interglacial.

Access and safety

It is recommended that the section shown in Photo 3 should be viewed through the boundary fence, and, because the site is really quite dangerous, the accessible portions should be traversed with great care. When traversing around the head of the site to visit the basal platform, take heed of the fence and warning notice. The seaward edge has a very thin bridge over an open joint: **do not** be tempted to explore or even attempt to photograph the feature. The site is now very dangerous.

THE SOUTH DORSET COAST

The South Dorset coast provides exceptionally fine geological walks and an ideal opportunity to examine the relationships between rock type, structure and landform (Table 1, Figure 1).

The dominant feature is the east–west structural alignment controlled by the Weymouth anticline and its extension through the coast as the Ham Cliff and Ringstead anticlines. There are important east–west faults through Redcliff Point (SY 712816) and Ringstead (SY 752814) and a Tertiary reversed fault at Bat's Head (SY 795803). The rock types are entirely sedimentary but involve a full range from **arenaceous** (sandy) to **argillaceous** (clayey), calcareous to ferruginous, and rapidly alternating sequences and thicknesses of clays, sand, limestones and evaporites (rocks created by the evaporation of salty waters) – sometimes cemented, often loose. Erosion patterns and rates vary over short distances to yield a succession of vertical cliffs, small bays, landslides, rock falls and intriguing evolutionary sequences (Figure 7). The exact type of process depends on the plan position of the coast in relation to the outcrop and structure. This is far too complex to describe in a short book and the interested reader of geology is referred to House (1989). For the geomorphology, it is suggested that the sites listed below are visited.

Weymouth Beach

Weymouth Beach (SY 683790) is discordant to the structure and has a fine marshland (Radipole Lake and Lodmoor Country Park), representing an infilled estuary, behind a fascinating beach. The beach material ranges in grain size from fine sands near the harbour to shingle and pebbles near Bowleaze Cove (SY 703819). In consequence there is a steady increase in beach slope but a decrease in width. This is a nice example of the way in which the properties of materials influence form. On the natural beach there is an almost perfect statistical relationship between these variables. The beach has now been much affected by artificial sand nourishment (at the harbour end) and by beach protection works (at its northern end). The most northerly point of Weymouth Beach is backed by the Oxford Clay cliffs at Furzy Cliff (SY 698818) and Bowleaze Cove. A sea wall has recently been constructed along a portion of this stretch and new properties have been built immediately behind it. It will be interesting to see how effective this sea wall is, especially where it ends, because the beach may retreat and cause the wall to be attacked from the side and rear. The mass movements between Bowleaze Cove and Redcliff Point (including large rotational slips) are currently active and are worth visiting.

Black Head and Osmington Mills

Black Head and Osmington Mills (SY 728820 and SY 734816) are important because the structure brings a thick sequence of the Kimmeridge Clay to the surface, overlain by the Upper Greensand and the Gault. A large landslide complex is thereby generated. The slides are currently active and demonstrate the mudslide process very clearly. The northward dip and the shallow slopes in the Kimmeridge concentrate the water flow to make this a favourite landslide visit. The location of the stream in relation to the structure is also worth examining. To the east the relationships between the Cretaceous and the Corallian can be seen as well as older landslide forms.

Ringstead to White Nothe

Ringstead to White Nothe (SY 752814 and SY 772808) is an interesting part to visit because a shallow fold brings the Chalk, Upper Greensand and Gault into contact with the Portland and Purbeck and then with the Kimmeridge. The result of this classic juxtaposition of permeable with impermeable beds is the famous, huge White Nothe landslide. This slide is controlled in location and outline by the structure. A further large, fault-guided slide occurs at Holworth (SY 764814).

Bat's Head to Durdle Door

Bat's Head to Durdle Door (SY 795803 and SY 805802) must not be missed. If the coastal walk cannot be managed, use the magnificent Durdle Door viewpoint. The Chalk reaches sea-level at

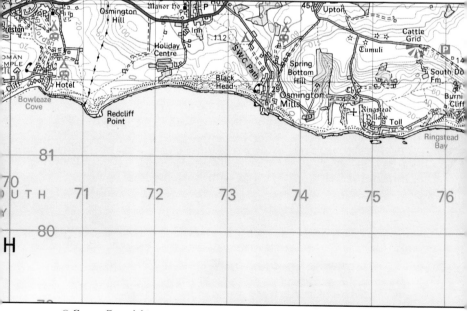

© Crown Copyright

White Nothe itself due to the regional dip and from there to Bat's Head, Swyre Head and Durdle Door there are some of the most beautiful chalk cliffs in England. They have an additional interest because they are carved out of resistant and near vertical chalk, in places overthrust and often cut by southward-dipping flexural shears. This presents an unusual attitude to the force of the sea and largely accounts for the vertical forms (Photo 4) and the small caves. The retreat of the cliffs has also left small chalk valleys hanging over the sea (eg. Scratchy Bottom, immediately to the west of Durdle Door). These contain fine residual soil deposits including soliflucted materials and buried soils. Due to the steep cliffs, however, most of these can only been seen from a distance. These fine cliffs continue through Dungy Head (SY 815800) to Lulworth (SY 825799) where the Wealden and the Portland and Purbeck Beds reappear.

Durdle Door itself is a natural arch cut in the near vertical Portland Stone, and the rocks, Blind Cow off Swyre Head and the Bull off Scratchy Bottom, are remnants of the Portland Stone barrier that becomes so important further to the east (Photo 5).

Scratchy Bottom

The dry valley of Scratchy Bottom which runs northward immediately to the west of Durdle Door can be approached by some steps that run up the cliff face at SY 803804. A bridlepath runs along much of its length up to Newlands Farm, thus providing easy access. Scratchy Bottom is a splendid location to consider the origin of dry valleys for it has an interesting morphology and some well exposed sediments where its course has been truncated by the cliffs.

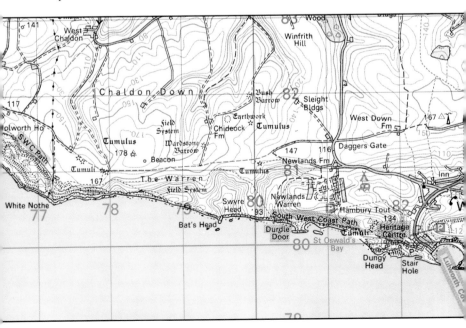

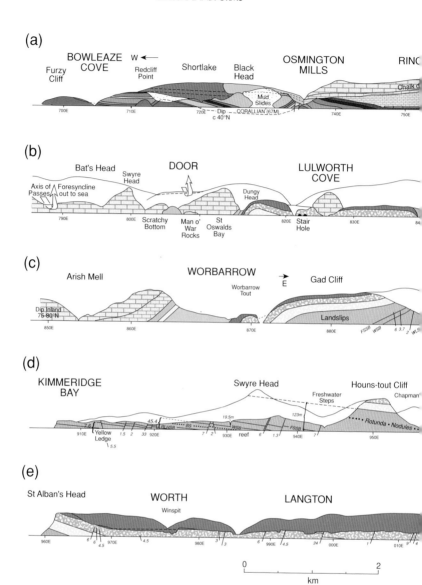

The morphology is of interest because of three characteristics: its sheer size, the presence of a right-angled bend starting at SY 803808, and the fact that it heads up to a watershed which is narrow and almost links up with dry valleys that run down into Lulworth Cove. An important question is why the valley is so large when it has such a small catchment area? One can also ask why it is so flat-bottomed, why it has a right-angled bend, and why its upper portions are so steep. Scratchy Bottom is undoubtedly a relict feature in the landscape for it currently has no stream channel, its course has been truncated at its lower end by cliff retreat, and the sediments on its side and bottom at its seaward end appear to be of some antiquity. They

24

Key

Upper Chalk	
Middle Chalk	
Lower Chalk	
Upper Greensand & Gault	
Purbeck Beds	
Portland Stone	
Portland Sandstone	
Kimmeridge Clay	
Osmington Oolite	
Sandsfoot Grits	
Bencliff Grit	
Preston Grit	
Northe Clay	
Northe Grit	
Trigonia Beds	
Oxford Clay	

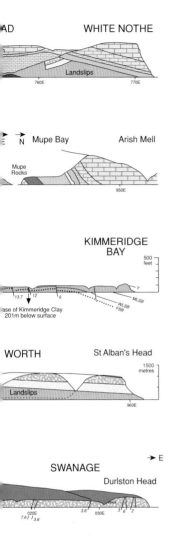

Figure 7: Sections illustrating the geology of the Dorset coast between Weymouth and Swanage.
(a) Furzy Cliff to White Nothe, (b) White Nothe to Arish Mell, (c) Arish Mell to Kimmeridge Bay, (d) Kimmeridge Bay to St Alban's Head, and (e) St Alban's Head to Durlston Head. From: House 1989.

would appear to be an example of scree or soliflucted material generated during cold conditions in the Pleistocene. Could it be that the dry valley was formed by severe frost shattering and runoff under cold conditions (when there was rapid runoff as a result of the melting of snow in the early summer and the chalk was sealed by permafrost) when this water ran across the surface rather than going underground as it does today? Alternatively, was the valley caused by a spring cutting back into the Chalk along a joint to produce the right-angled bend and to excavate the steep headwall at the landward end of the valley? Scratchy Bottom is a perplexing but dramatic landform about which there are many unanswered questions. Table 2 lists some of the

Photo 4: Shore platform and rock fall to west of Durdle Door.
Photo: Andrew Goudie.

Photo 5: The South Dorset Coast at Durdle Door.
Photo: Sillson Communications, Wareham.

Table 2: Dry valley hypotheses

Uniformitarian
Events of high magnitude and low frequency, ie. floods
Developments of permeability through time
Stripping of surface cover through time
Scarp retreat through time
River capture
Downcutting of master stream through time

Climate change
Permafrost
Glacial erosion
Nival regimes
Glacial meltwater
Increased rainfall
Mass movement acceleration
Reduced evapotranspiration

Base-level change
Raised submarine canyons
Eustatic
Tectonic
Isostatic

Anthropogenic
Vegetation change
Groundwater abstraction

many hypotheses that have been put forward over the years to explain the dry valley systems of southern Britain. It is worth considering in the field which of these might explain the origin of Scratchy Bottom.

Access and safety
Weymouth Beach and the South Dorset coast can be easily seen from the sea front.

Black Head and **Osmington Mills** can be reached from the private car park at Osmington Mills (SY 734817).

Ringstead to White Nothe is best viewed from the track leading from the car park west of Holworth House. There is a zigzag path down the cliff near the old coastguard station. Great care is required. It is not suitable for field parties or pranksters.

Bat's Head to Durdle Door should be treated as a coastal footpath walk with viewpoints and no cliff scrambling. The view and descent to the beach at Durdle Door will be sufficient to please most people.

Durdle Door and **Scratchy Bottom** can be reached in two ways. After turning off the road from Winfrith Newburgh to West Lulworth at Newlands Farm (SY 811810), park at the car park at the end of the caravan site and then follow the marked coastal path. This car park is only accessible by car or minibus. The alternative is to follow the footpath from the Lulworth Cove car park westward over Dungy Head along the footpath above St Oswald's Bay.

The sea cliffs and rock slopes of the entire area are very precipitous and subject to rockfall. They are extremely dangerous and must not be climbed. Rockfalls do occur from the promontories and from the chalk cliffs.

THE LULWORTH COAST

Photo 6: Lulworth Cove. *Photo: Sillson Communications, Wareham.*

The Lulworth coast is probably the most frequently visited, poorly described, and least understood of all the famous geological and geomorphological teaching sites on the British coastline (Photo 6).

Lulworth Cove is used for teaching exercises because it is held to illustrate two general principles – namely, that stage of development is an important consideration in understanding landforms and that it is possible to use sequences of landforms to illustrate change through time. It is not possible for us to study the evolution of a landscape from its beginning to a fully developed form because the processes of erosion and deposition generally act too slowly for their work to be observed in a lifetime. Sometimes, however, a sequence of forms in space occurs and if the forms are controlled by similar conditions, they can be arranged in a time-based series from oldest to youngest (Burt and Goudie 1994). This idea is often applied to the coastline between Durdle Door and Worbarrow Tout (SY 869795), for along the coast there is a series of coves, partially or completely developed in similar rocks, which appear to be different stages of the same process.

Thus it is believed that Stair Hole (SY 823798) represents the beginning of a new bay, that Lulworth Cove is an intermediate but beautifully developed feature (as near perfect as can be conceived) and that Mupe Bay, Worbarrow Bay and Man O'War Cove at Durdle Door represent a condition where the original geological controls have been all but destroyed and several coves have merged so that the curved cove form is lost and a new system comes into play.

This idea rests on an understanding of the geology (Figure 8), for there is a distribution inland of Late Jurassic to Upper Cretaceous rocks parallel to the coastline. The Jurassic consists of Portland and Purbeck rocks, which are predominantly limestones but with some softer bands. The beds are very steeply dipping and contorted and present a resistant rampart towards the forces of the sea. Behind them occur less resistant Cretaceous rocks comprising Wealden Clays, the Upper Greensand and the Gault, which are more easily eroded. In turn, behind these lie the more massive escarpment of the Chalk which tends to form a prominent escarpment, high hills and steep slopes inland.

The argument applied to explain the supposed development sequence is that the sea fights to penetrate the coastal barrier of limestone, breaches it in narrow arches (Stair Hole) which collapse to form entrances to small bays and then, when it reaches the soft Wealden Beds, causes rapid erosion so that a wide, near-circular symmetrical bay (Lulworth) develops behind a narrow entrance. The beauty of the cove is enhanced by the difference of relief between the coastal barrier and the steep white cliffs of chalk behind. Once the cove has reached the Chalk the development of the bay becomes slower than the widening of the mouth. Progressively the Portland and Purbeck Beds are destroyed until only small **stacks** and partly submerged reefs remain. Examples are the lines of rocks known as Man O'War Rocks and Mupe Rocks. At this point shore erosion becomes very important and the bay widens out at its mouth, perhaps to merge with neighbouring bays and to form a straighter coastline. Thus Worbarrow Bay and St Oswald's Bay form an elongated double bay by the amalgamation of two former coves comparable in form and origin (if not scale) with Lulworth. The coast to the west of Durdle Door, which appears to have been the result of the amalgamation of up to three coves, represents the final stages of the sequence. The limestone barrier has almost disappeared with only the Bull, Calf and Cow rocks exposed at low tide. (For this local detail see the Ordnance Survey 1:25 000 map.)

There are several problems with this appealing teaching model. It is not possible to apply the space-for-time substitution too rigorously because the rock conditions are not, in fact, so similar that equal times of development would apply to each portion of the coast. The outcrops of the 'parallel beds' in fact widen towards the east (Figure 8). Thus it would have taken longer for Worbarrow Bay to develop and successively less time for the bays towards Durdle Door, and yet in reality the bays at Durdle Door and Worbarrow are both

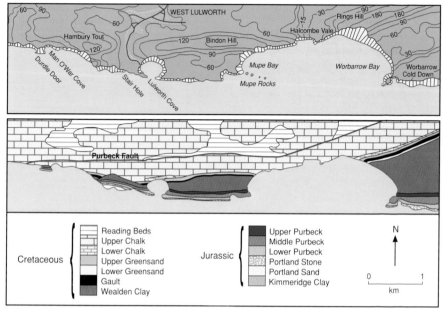

Figure 8: The topography, location and geology of the Dorset coast at Durdle Door, *Stair Hole, Lulworth and Worbarrow Bay.*

developed almost to destruction where the beds are in turn both narrowest and widest.

Several other factors must be taken into account. All of the bays are fed by very big valley systems, some of which carry perennial streams for part of their length. These valleys are much too large to have been formed after the breaching of the coastal limestone barrier and therefore the rivers which created them must have flowed out to sea through a valley in the Portland and Purbeck Stone. In other words, it is not necessary for marine breaching to occur before a bay can develop. In this sense Stair Hole is unique in that it does not possess a valley system and so should, perhaps, be considered a completely separate case. It is the view of the authors that Lulworth Cove probably represents a partially submerged or drowned river valley (or **ria**) which has been trimmed into a near-circular shape by fluvial and mass movement activity (Figure 9). The same interpretation is also probably true of Worbarrow Bay.

It is not known how the development of the coast was affected by the high sea-levels of the last interglacial which formed the Portland raised beaches between 9-15m OD. There are beaches at the mouth of Lulworth and Stair Hole at this height and so the sea may have flooded the area. There is a notch above the Lulworth ice cream cafe at the same height but it is not known if this is of marine origin.

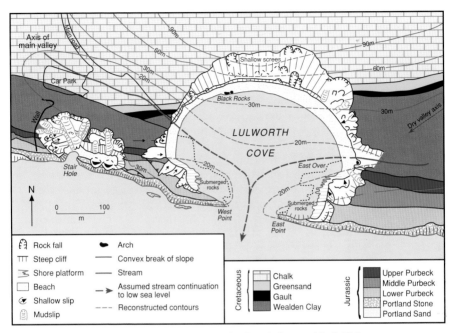

Figure 9: The geology and geomorphology of Lulworth Cove and Stair Hole.
On the eastern side the Wealden Clay is followed by a dry valley system. The two valleys, once united, formed a single stream which crossed the coastal rock ridge between West and East Points.

What is certain, however, is that the streams would once have flowed to the lower sea-levels of the glacial periods through the mouth at Lulworth or across Worbarrow Bay. A combination of this and the greater runoff of colder times means that these streams may have had a high erosional energy and would have easily opened a deep gorge through what is now the coastal barrier. At this time the chalk and Wealden Beds would have formed valley-side slopes covered in weathered debris and affected by solifluction and other mass movement processes. Evidence for this can be seen in thick sections of head behind the cottages on the north side of the road as the Cove is approached. Sections of head, in the first cliff edge to the north of the stream, can also be observed from the beach. Here, up to 1m of fine, chalky head or **coombe rock** overlies the Greensand and Chalk.

Further around the Cove, shallow scree-slope remnants hang precariously on the chalk cliffs and are today being steadily removed by erosion. These are much better developed on the valley slopes which lead into the firing range on the eastern side of the bay. They are believed to represent the original form of the Lulworth valley before drowning by the sea. As the sea-level rose again in the post-glacial period after the last glaciation the lower part of the cliffs within the Cove was trimmed by the sea into the perfect shape we know today. This was assisted by rapid mass movement on the Wealden Beds and the present slopes on these deposits are scored by many slumps, gullies and mudslides. A perfect example exists on its eastern side (East Over) (Figure 9) with a new arcuate scar. It is felt that a similar argument can be applied to Worbarrow Bay.

Stair Hole does not possess a valley system and is developing by the classic model that proposes coastal breaching by wave action. The sea has almost reached the soft Wealden Beds and is about to begin widening a bay towards the Lulworth road; it is certainly removing any debris brought down to the cove. It is important to notice that the cliff erosion and cove widening are being brought about by landslides and mudslides rather than by direct marine erosion (Figure 9). These slides are beautifully developed forms with source areas at the head, long tracks with lateral shear zones, crevasses as they tumble into the cove, and, during winter, muddy lobes across the boulder beach below. With time, a bay similar to those at Durdle Door and Mupe Bay will develop as the Stair Hole arches are reduced to the isolated stacks seen at Man O'War Rocks and Mupe Rocks. Thus the true teaching sequence is Stair Hole–Durdle Door–Mupe Rocks–Man O'War Rocks. The greatest interest, however, lies in the complex fluvial, mass movement, climate change and sea-level change history displayed at Lulworth.

At many points along the South Dorset coast there are well developed landforms called 'shore platforms' (see Photo 4). These are relatively flat rock surfaces developed in the intertidal zone. Whether these features are exposed to view depends very much on the state of the tide and on whether or not the beach is currently undergoing sediment deposition or removal. In the past these features have often been termed 'wavecut platforms', but this makes the assumption that the prime or only process involved in their formation is planation by wave attack. However, as Table 3 illustrates, there are in fact likely to be many factors involved in the formation and character of a shore platform besides wave abrasion. These include the role of weathering processes such as salt attack, frost action and solution. The platforms

Table 3: Shore platforms: mechanisms of formation

Wave abrasion	
Weathering	– salt
	– frost
	– solution
Biological processes	– boring organisms, etc.
	– grazing
Structural control	– benches related to hard rocks and the presence of bedding planes
	– fault and joint control

may also be modified extensively by biological processes such as boring, grazing and armouring by barnacles, molluscs, etc. Finally, the platforms may be the result primarily of controls exerted by the **lithology** and structure. (There is no finer exposition of this than the extension fault and joint fractures at Kimmeridge Bay (Photo 7).) In other words, they may result from the presence of a bed of resistant rock outcropping in the intertidal zone.

Access and safety

Lulworth is reached by the B3071 road from Wool or the B3070 from Holmebridge (SY 891870). Visitors should park in the official car park at SY 822800 just before the road descends to the beach, as direct vehicle access is not permitted to the Cove itself. There are signposts at this car park to Stair Hole and Lulworth. Lulworth now has an Interpretation Centre and information and teaching services are available by arrangement. Remember to tell the person at the gate if you are an educational party.

The sea cliffs and rock slopes of the entire area are very precipitous and subject to rockfall. They are extremely dangerous and must not be climbed. Rockfalls do occur from the promontories and from the chalk cliffs within Lulworth Cove, where people have recently been killed. Please exercise care. The mudslides in Stair Hole and Lulworth Cove are generally slippery rather than deep.

Mupe Bay and Worbarrow Bay can be accessed only by footpath from the eastern side of Lulworth Cove through the firing range gates. Yellow-topped posts should be followed in this area and signposted safety instructions meticulously observed.

THE EAST PURBECK COAST

This area is sometimes called the Isle of Purbeck and, like West Dorset, it contains walks and viewpoints of Heritage Coast class. The geology of this coast is world famous, but in other respects it has received relatively little attention. In what follows here, the focus is on selected themes and locations of particular interest which can be explored by visitors to the area.

The main theme, as with the Weymouth to Durdle Door coast, is the relationship of the coastal forms to the structure and lithology of the rocks. In this case, however, there are added ingredients because the area lies on the northern limb of the Purbeck anticline which is very broad and asymmetrical (Figure 10).

The coastline between Lulworth and Kimmeridge (Photo 7) is parallel to the structure and the outcrop is very narrow due to the eastward thinning of the beds and the effect of the Purbeck monocline

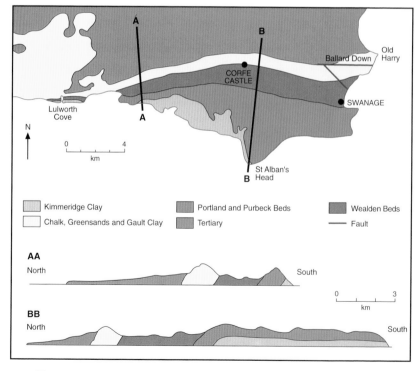

Figure 10: The geology and structure of the Isle of Purbeck.
After: Steers (in Whittow 1992).

Photo 7: Kimmeridge Bay. *Photo: Sillson Communications, Wareham.*

Photo 8: St Alban's Head. *Photo: Sillson Communications, Wareham.*

Photo 9: The cliffs and shore platform at Kimmeridge. *Photo: Andrew Goudie.*

outcrop. Eastward the coast turns south-east as far as St Alban's Head (SY 961754) (Photo 8) then runs north of east to Durlston Head (SZ 034772) and north-south to Studland (SZ 034825). The coast crosses toward the plunging and narrowing termination of the Purbeck anticline where the beds are becoming more horizontal and wider apart (Figure 2). The Purbeck Beds become a structural plateau surface with the Portland Beds presenting massive rampart cliffs to the sea. The cliffs of St Alban's Head are some of the most inaccessible on the south coast. Toward Durlston, elevation and rocks descend with the dip to bring less resistant rocks toward sea-level and the height of the cliffs thereby diminishes. The Portland Stone still forms the lower vertical cliffs but there is now a slope-over-wall form. In contrast, the Kimmeridge to Chapman's Pool reach is noted for the type sections of Kimmeridge Clay (Photo 9) and it will not escape the attention of the visitor that once again classic landslide conditions occur. It comes as no surprise, therefore, to find such great failures at Chapman's Pool (SY 956772) where there is a deep-seated slide and many mudslides and rockfalls. There are also deep-seated slides at St Albans Head, Houns-tout (SY 951773) and Gad Cliff (SY 885795), and Worbarrow Bay was the location of a modern landslide monitoring station (Allison and Brunsden 1990). Regular falls of rock occur all along this coast and Durlston Bay has been closed because of the resulting danger. Rates of cliff retreat are rapid (Table 4). The foreshore is affected by several faults and there is a fine development of shore platforms and limestone ledges. Here, the rhythmic rock sequence of clay, shale, limestone dominates the landforming

Table 4: Some average rates of cliff retreat in Dorset

Location	metres per 100 years
Furzy Cliff-Shortlake (Oxford Clay)	37
Ringstead (Kimmeridge Clay)	41
White Nothe-Hambury Tout (Chalk)	21
Kimmeridge Bay (Kimmeridge Clay)	39
Ballard Down (Chalk)	23
Worbarrow Bay (Wealden Beds)	56

Source: Goudie 1995.

controls; every hard and resistant rock forms a ledge, barrier or 'Head', and every clay a weakness to be exploited.

At Durlston (Figure 11) the conditions change again. So far we have been dealing with a concordant coast but here the coast is discordant to the structures. The response is dramatic and predictable with the resistant beds forming headlands and the erodible materials being rapidly removed to form bays. In this case the process is aided by the steady increase in width of the Wealden Beds which form Swanage Bay between the headlands of Peveril Point and Ballard Down (SZ 040786 and SZ 045814).

Durlston shows steeply dipping, faulted Portland Stone followed by cliffs in the Broken Beds, the Cockle Beds and the type section of the Purbeck. Ballard Down at Foreland Point is simply spectacular with steeply north-dipping chalk forming irregular but vertical cliffs, The Pinnacles and Old Harry Rocks (Photo 10). These stacks, which are among the most ephemeral of landforms, always catch the eye. A common explanation of stacks is that they are produced by coastal erosion which exploits weakness to form a sea cave or arch which then collapses to yield a mere stump. For arches to develop, however, requires quite special requirements. They are similar to tunnels when they are formed, which means that they must be able to resist the compressive forces of the overburden materials. As the surrounding rocks are worn away they become, like Durdle Door, more like bridges in which either there is a beam supported on piers or there is a 'triangular' keystone locking the centre of the arch. In both cases the load of the supported material must be transferred down the supports in such a way that there are no 'sideways' effects, otherwise the arch would fall. It is perhaps significant that many arches tend toward a perfect parabolic form because, left alone with no further erosion at the base, the parabola is one of the most stable forms in nature. It was often used by early engineers to create such masterpieces as the early Roman viaducts. As usual, natural design is first and best!

At Ballard Point (SZ 049813) the sea has to exploit steeply dipping faults, joints or bedding planes which preclude the development of an arch because there is nothing to support it or to provide a keystone.

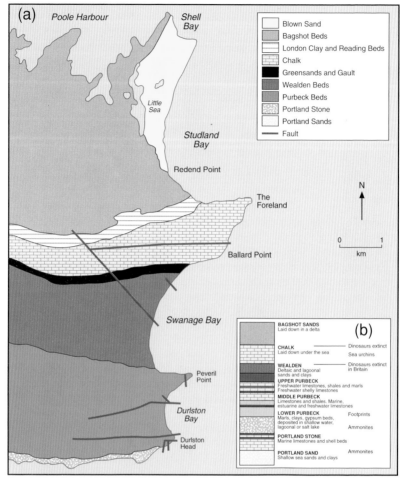

Figure 11: The eastern Isle of Purbeck: (a) geology and structure and
(b) main rock types.

As a result, the middle falls to leave pinnacles. At Ballard Cliff this
takes place in an environment with erosion rates of 0.23m per year
measured between 1882-1962.

The last point to emphasise is the effect of the change in dip of the
rocks on the northern margin of the Isle of Purbeck, known as the
Purbeck monocline. At Ballard Down the rocks dip steeply to the
north-east, forming a structure discordant to the processes. Westward,
towards Worbarrow, this dip steadily increases so that when the rocks
next meet the sea they present a formidable planar, concordant bastion
which has to be breached before a discordant erodible face can again
be developed in the thin Wealden Beds. The thinning of all the beds
means that the barrier is of flimsy construction. The fact that it
presents to the sea an anti-dip face of Portland Stone (Figure 11) is the
cause of the resistance and the peculiar coastal forms.

Photo 10: Old Harry Rocks. *Photo: Sillson Communications, Wareham.*

To progress, the sea must undercut the dip-slope to cause block-and-wedge rockfalls. In fact, as the dip changes so does the fracture pattern and the rock strength. In the east the detachment is mainly by falls of rectangular blocks (Tilly Whim (SZ 031770) and Emmett's Hill (SY 958765)). Near Kimmeridge and Worbarrow Bays wedge failures are common and further west toppling failures become more and more common. Once the sea or rivers have breached the barrier to open up the inland facing-back (dip) slope it is then possible to get dip-slope planar slides. That is the process, for example, at Stair Hole. The dip of the rocks increases to the west becoming nearly vertical at Durdle Door and in the chalk beyond it is overturned. This sequence of relationships is one of the best teaching examples of 'rocks and relief' in the world.

There are many other interesting features on the Purbeck coast. For example, at Seacombe Cliff (SY 984766) there is a section in the valley bottom which shows a thick accumulation of frost-shattered valley fill of Pleistocene age. However, perhaps the most striking feature of this stretch of coastline, apart from the relationship between geology and landform, is the role that humans have played in slope modification. The valley-side slopes show some of the finest examples of ancient terraced field systems, called lynchets, to be found anywhere in the British Isles (Photo 11). Many of these may be of medieval age, for in medieval time parallel strip lynchets were created by ploughing as population pressures forced cultivation to take place on high angle slopes. Or are the instincts of the second author more correct in thinking they are ancient vineyards?

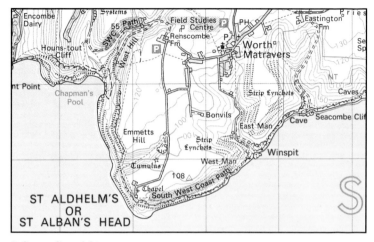

© Crown Copyright

Access

The coast to the south of Worth Matravers (SY 974775) is easily accessible and provides many excellent opportunities to examine the Portland Beds. These have been extensively quarried and mined at both Winspit (SY 977761) and Seacombe Cliff.

Photo 11: Strip lynchets near Worth Matravers. Photo: Andrew Goudie.

STUDLAND BAY AND THE SOUTH HAVEN PENINSULA

To the west and north of Studland village, and projecting into the entrance to Poole Harbour, is the South Haven Peninsula. Much of it is occupied by the Studland Heath National Nature Reserve which was established to protect some ecologically valuable heathland habitat, much of which has disappeared from other parts of southern England. Background historical information is provided by Legg (1987).

To the geomorphologist (and the biogeographer) the appeal of the Peninsula is that it is an area with a well-attested history of coastal change and dune evolution. Before about 1600 the coastline of Studland Bay was considerably to the west of its present position and probably consisted of a low cliff of Tertiary sands and gravels (the Bagshot Beds). Since that time the coast has built out seawards by about 800-850m in the north and by 300-350m in the south. A sequence of dunes and inter-dune depressions (slacks) has developed, the latter now being occupied by lakes and swamps. As the dunes have developed, so lagoons have been formed, and these have gradually become isolated from the sea to produce freshwater lakes known as Little Sea and Eastern Lake (Figure 12).

Four main dunes have been recognised and they have been dated by using old maps and charts (Figure 13). The westernmost ridge, conventionally called Third Ridge, seems to have been more or less completed by the 1720s. The second dune complex, Second Ridge, began to form considerably further seaward leaving a wide slack now known as Central Marsh. It seems to have been fully developed by the 1840s. First Ridge had formed by about 1900. Since the 1950s the most seaward ridge, Zero Ridge, has formed. It is still actively developing, and bare sand is widespread. This is in contrast to the older ridges, which are now for the most part vegetated, though even they suffer some sand movement and blowout development. The area was a military training area during the Second World War and some of the blowouts date back to that time. Subsequent mine clearance at the end of the war involved clearing the greater part of the vegetation (Ranwell and Boar 1986).

The dunes are subjected to considerable visitor pressure but have nonetheless not been degraded to the same extent as many in the British Isles. The possibility and consequences of fire are reduced by careful management and regular warden patrols, and access is restricted to the two ends of the system so that the central part is relatively unaffected, even though as many as 15 000 people may visit the site on a sunny summer Sunday. Because of its sheltered location

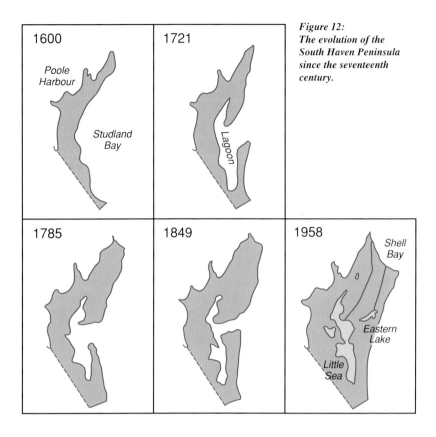

Figure 12:
The evolution of the
South Haven Peninsula
since the seventeenth
century.

and an adequate source of sand to replenish the beach, the dunes appear to be naturally robust.

The dated sequence of dunes shown in Figure 13 presents an excellent laboratory to see how dune form, dune soils and dune vegetation evolve through time – a process ecologists call 'succession'. In a transect, (Figure 14) one moves westwards along the line of Cross Track from the steep, active crest of Zero Ridge which is essentially yellow in colour and alkaline in pH, and with a vegetation assemblage dominated by grasses that thrive in a rapidly accreting environment (eg. *Ammophila arenaria* and *Elymus arctus*), to dunes that have an increasing degree of soil development, organic horizon accumulation, and tree and shrub cover (eg. gorse, bracken, birch and pine).

Access and safety
The best place to do a transect across the South Haven dunes is along the track that runs east-south-eastwards from the road to SZ 034862. Parking is available on the road side. In the slacks it can be wet underfoot so wellington boots are recommended. Please do not light fires (the heathlands are highly combustible) and watch out for nudists and snakes, both of which inhabit the area!

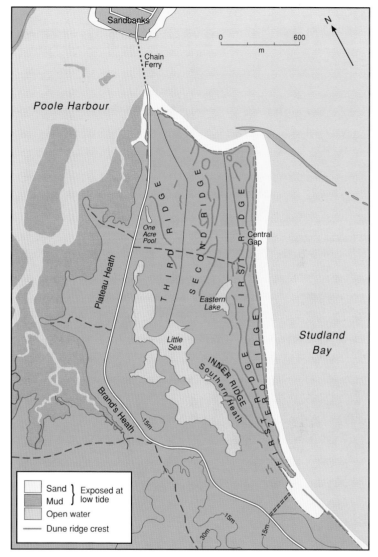

Figure 13: The main dune ridges of the South Haven Peninsula. After: Carr 1971.

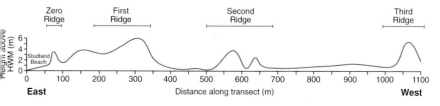

Figure 14: Transect across the dunes of South Haven Peninsula.

POOLE HARBOUR

Poole Harbour (Figure 15 and Photo 12) is a particularly good location to see the way in which sediment accumulation, creek pattern and vegetation type are inter-related. The Harbour covers approximately 4000ha, of which 80% is occupied by intertidal mudflats. It has a shoreline approaching 150km in length, and a narrow opening to the sea which is crossed by the Studland–Sandbanks chain ferry and used by large cross-Channel ferries. The tidal range at spring tides is between 0.4 and 2.2m.

The Harbour is a drowned river valley into which the rivers Frome and Piddle currently flow. The drowning was caused by the post-glacial rise in sea-level (the Flandrian Transgression) and was more or less complete 5-6000 years ago. Since that time the Harbour has become progressively silted up and mudflats and saltmarshes have developed. This sedimentation process was accelerated in the late nineteenth century when a hybrid grass, *Spartina anglica*, invaded the

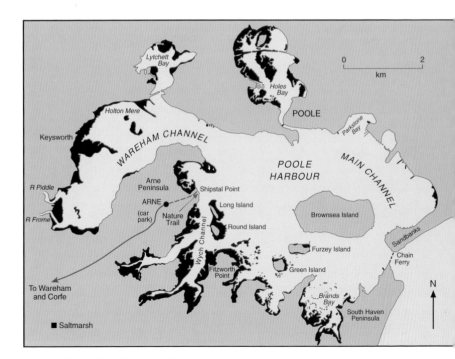

Figure 15: Saltmarsh in Poole Harbour.

Photo 12: A view of Poole Harbour *looking towards Sandbanks, with the South Haven peninsula on the right. Photo: Andrew Goudie.*

native marsh vegetation. The significance of this event has been summarised by Bird:

> 'A century ago Poole Harbour had relatively narrow fringing salt marshes and wide soft mudflats exposed at low tide. The salt-tolerant rice (cord) grass, *Spartina anglica*, which had developed as the result of hybridisation between the native *Spartina maritima* and accidentally introduced American rice grass, *Spartina alterniflora* in Southampton Water in the 1870s, became established in Poole Harbour in 1899. It quickly spread across intertidal areas that had previously been soft mud sparsely vegetated with patches of eel grass (*Zostera* spp), trapping muddy sediment and converting them into grassy marshland. This resulted in the building of broad marshland terraces up close to high tide mark, while the intervening creeks and tidal channels became narrower and deeper' (Bird 1995, p. 192).

The role of vegetation in marsh accretion is indeed fundamental, and as vegetation colonises mudflats, so the mudflats become higher as the vegetation traps more sediment. This in turn enables other plants, less tolerant of salinity and immersion, to colonise the marsh surface, and so the building up process continues until the surface is effectively less and less prone to tidal inundation. At that point freshwater species (eg. sedges) become increasingly important. This is a further example of the succession process.

45

Although many of the *Spartina* areas around Poole Harbour appear to be in a healthy state, there has in fact been a reduction in *Spartina* extent in recent decades as a result of a process called die-back. The process started as early as the 1920s and has been especially serious in the marshes lying eastward off Shipstal Point and Arne. The degradation of the *Spartina* swards seems to begin at the edges, and with the widening and coalescence of marsh channels increasingly fragmented islets separated by a reticulate pattern of mud are produced. Such degradation has been observed at many other marsh sites in southern Britain (Doody 1984), but the reasons are still not clear. Wave attack could have become more severe because of changes in climate conditions or the disturbance caused by bow waves from boats and ships. Rising sea-levels may also have contributed. Alternatively, it may be that as the marshes get older, so the sediments become more beset by waterlogged and anaerobic conditions that the *Spartina* finds distasteful.

Access and safety

A good view of Poole Harbour (Photo 12) can be obtained from a lay-by on the B3351 near the golf course to the west of Studland (SZ 016818). To see the marsh itself take the footpath from Arne to Shipstal Point (SY 983884). Saltmarshes and mudflats are dangerous; you can sink in. Please also be careful not to disturb the many birds that inhabit the marshes, heaths and mudflats. At Arne there is a car park and a nature trail managed by the Royal Society for the Protection of Birds.

GLOSSARY

Amino acid racemisation A dating technique based on the fact that protein preserved in the skeletal remains of animals (including shells) undergoes a series of chemical reactions, many of which are time dependent.

Aquiclude A porous rock which, although usually permeable, becomes impermeable because of the saturation of its pores by water.

Arenaceous Pertaining to, containing or composed of sand.

Argillaceous Pertaining to, containing or composed of clay.

Chert Layers or irregular concretions of silica occurring, usually, in limestone and sandy formations.

Coombe rock A structureless mass of unweathered and largely unrolled, but often broken, flints embedded in a matrix of chalky paste and disintegrated chalk, moved downslope by solifluction.

Freestone Easily carved stone.

Glauconitic Materials containing a mineral called glauconite.

Graben A valley or trough produced by faulting and subsidence or by uplift of adjacent rock masses (Horsts).

Head A deposit similar to Coombe Rock in origin but formed on bedrocks other than chalk. Also a coastal headland.

Imbrication The structure resulting from the piling one upon another or individual rock particles, like the partly overlapping tiles of a roof.

Involution The results of frost action in the upper soil layers.

Lithology The general character of a rock, particularly as seen in field exposures and hand specimens.

Overconsolidated A material that has been subjected to a great pressure by the overburden of material on top of it.

Periglacial The zone surrounding or bordering the glacial zone and one in which frost action is important.

Ria A river valley that has been submerged by the sea.

Scree An accumulation of mainly angular material which lies at an angle of about 35° beneath an exposed cliff or free face. The principal cause of deposition is rockfall.

Solifluction The wholesale movement, in cold regions, of an upper, wet (thawed) layer of material over frozen or otherwise impermeable ground.

Stack A high rock pillar off the coast, detached from the main cliff by erosion, particularly applicable if the rock is precipitous, columnar and has regular more or less horizontal strata.

BIBLIOGRAPHY

Allison, R.J. (1989) 'Rates and mechanisms of change in hard rock coastal cliffs' in *Zeitschrift für Geomorphologie*, NF 73, 125-38.

Allison, R.J. and Brunsden, D. (1990) 'Some mudslide movement patterns' in *Earth Surface Processes and Landforms*, 15, 297-311.

Arkell, W.J. (1947) *The Geology of the Country Around Weymouth, Swanage, Corfe and Lulworth*. HMSO, Memoirs of the Geological Survey, London.

Barber, K.E. (1987) *Wessex and Isle of Wight Field Guide*. Quaternary Research Association, Cambridge.

Bird, E.C.F. (1995) *Geology and Scenery of Dorset*. Ex Libris, Bradford-on-Avon.

Brunsden, D., Coombe, E.D.K., Goudie, A.S. and Parker, A.G. (1996) 'The structural geomorphology of the Isle of Portland, southern England' in *Proceedings of the Geologists' Association*, 107, 209-30.

Burt, T. and Goudie, A. (1994) 'Timing shape and shaping time' in *Geography Review*, 8(2), 25-9.

Burton, H.St.J. (1937) 'The origin of Lulworth Cove' in *Geological Magazine*, 74, 377-83.

Carr, A.P. (1971) 'South Haven Peninsula: physiographic changes in the twentieth century' in *Captain Cyril Diver, A Memoir*. Nature Conservancy Council, Furzebrook, 32-7.

Davies, G.M. (1956) *The Dorset Coast: A geological guide* (second edition). A.C. Black, London.

Davis, K.H. and Keen, D.H. (1985) 'The age of Pleistocene marine deposits at Portland, Dorset' in *Proceedings of the Geologists' Association*, 96, 217-25.

Diver, C. (1933) 'The physiography of South Haven Peninsula, Studland Heath, Dorset' in *Geographical Journal*, 81, 404-27.

Donovan, D.T. and Stride, A.H. (1961) 'An acoustic survey of the sea floor south of Dorset and its geological interpretation' in *Philosophical Transactions of the Royal Society*, 244, 299-330.

Doody, P. (ed) (1984) *Spartina Anglica in Great Britain*. Nature Conservancy Council, Huntingdon.

Goudie, A. (1995) *The Changing Earth*. Blackwell, Oxford.

Horsfall, D. (1993) 'Geological controls on coastal morphology' in *Geography Review*, 7(1), 16-22.

Hounsell, S.S.B. (1952) 'Portland and its stone' in *Mine Quarry Engineering*, 18, 107-11.

House, M. (1989) 'Geology of the Dorset coast', *A Geologists' Association Guide* No. 22.

Jones, M.E., Allison, R.J. and Gilligan, J. (1984) 'On the relationship between geology and coastal landform in central southern England' in *Proceedings of the Dorset Natural History and Archaeology Society*, 105, 107-18.

Keen, D.H. (1985) 'Late Pleistocene deposits and mollusca from Portland, Dorset' in *Geological Magazine*, 122, 181-6.

Legg, R. (1987) *Purbeck's Heath. Claypits, nature and the oilfield*. Dorset Publishing, Sherborne.

May, V.J. (1971) 'The retreat of chalk cliffs' in *Geographical Journal*, 137, 203-6.

May, V.J. and Heeps, C. (1985) 'The nature and rate of change of chalk coastlines' in *Zeitschrift für Geomorphologie*, NF 57, 81-94.

Perkins, W.J. (1977) *Geology explained in Dorset*. David and Charles, Newton Abbot.

Prestwich, J. (1975) 'Notes on the phenomena of the Quaternary period on the Isle of Portland and round Weymouth' in *Quarterly Journal of the Geological Society*, 35, 29-54.

Pugh, M.E. and Shearman, D.J. (1967) 'Cryoturbation structures at the south end of the Isle of Portland' in *Proceedings of the Geologists' Association*, 78, 463-71.

Ranwell, D.S. and Boar, R. (1986) *Coastal Dune Management Guide*. Institute of Terrestrial Ecology, Huntingdon.

Whittow, J. (1992) *Geology and Scenery in Britain*. Chapman and Hall, London.

Wilson, K. (1960) 'The time factor in the development of dune soils at South Haven Peninsula, Dorset' in *Journal of Ecology*, 48, 341-59.